Steven Michael Grudzien

Choosing Kindness

(A big brother's advice on diversity, and how small acts of kindness are never small)

Based on a True Story

AuthorHouse™
1663 Liberty Drive
Bloomington, IN 47403
www.authorhouse.com
Phone: 1 (800) 839-8640

Published by AuthorHouse 08/21/2018

ISBN: 978-1-5462-4205-5 (sc)
ISBN: 978-1-5462-4204-8 (e)

Library of Congress Control Number: 2018905774

Print information available on the last page.

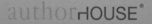

Story based on true events and written by
Steven Michael Grudzien
Woodbury, CT.

The illustrators of the book are:

Emily Ann Grudzien
Thea Eve Alfes
Linda Coon

A special thanks to:

Bethlehem Elementary School
Nonnewaug High School
The Zulpa Family
The Searles Family
The Williamson Family
Mrs. Judy Perruccci

Edited by Thea Eve Alfes with the help of Rita Cole.

It was a nice day to walk to the bus stop. Steve offered to get his little brother, Richard, off the bus. Richard liked when his brother came to get him off the bus. Playing football and wrestling took up a lot of Steve's time, so when the springtime came, Steve liked to do things for Richard.

Richard was quiet all the way home. When they got inside, Steve asked, "What's wrong Richard?"

"I have a problem!" Richard said.

Richard told Steve there was a new girl in school. She had just moved here with her family. "The teacher said she was from Poland," said Richard. "Some of the kids are making fun of how she talks. I wanted to include her in our baseball game at recess, but it was just us boys, and they said she couldn't play. She sat by herself," Richard exclaimed, "and she looked so sad."

Steve sat down with Richard. "You know, when we first moved here, you were just a baby. I was the new kid in school. I was overweight back then, and kids made fun of me." Steve put his hand on Richard's shoulder. "I was sad." Steve paused for a moment and added, "Then, I made a friend, and he included me at recess. My weight made me different from the other kids until someone had the courage to say that it didn't. I wound up being a pretty good football player."

Richard couldn't believe it. "You were the new kid? You were different? How could that be?" asked Richard. His brother had so many friends. His brother was the captain of his wrestling team. It was hard to imagine his big brother not being included in any games at recess.

"Richard," Steve sighed. "What's this new girls' name?"

Richard answered, "Her name is Alexandra. She has long brown hair, and she likes to draw!"

"Don't you like to draw too?" Steve asked.

"Yes," said Richard.

"Well then, you are the same," said Steve.

Richard knew what he had to do, but he wondered how he would do it. It wasn't just that Alexandra was new or that she spoke differently. It was also that she was a GIRL!

Girls had never played baseball with the boys before. When Alexandra asked if she could play, she was laughed at. Richard knew she felt bad.

Richard thought hard.

Steve knew exactly what Richard was thinking. "Richard, I'm going to tell you a true story."

"You mean it really happened?" asked Richard.

"It really happened," said Steve. "I learned an important lesson about a small act of kindness."

"What do you mean?" asked Richard. "What did you have to do?"

"There was a new girl in my school, just like Alexandra. Her name was Abby. She was from another state and didn't know anyone. She wanted to play football, but there was no girl's football team. Only boys played. She joined the team and no one spoke to her. No one sat with her. They ignored her. She was sad."

"One day, I decided to go sit with her. She was different than me because she was a girl and I was a boy, but that didn't make her bad. She was actually pretty good at football and she worked really hard in practice."

"I made her laugh!" said Steve. "It was the first time I'd seen her smile since she got to our school. I asked her to come sit at my table, with the other football players. After all, she was one of us."

"She came to our table, and she has been sitting with us ever since. My friends saw me include her, and they did too."

Steve paused for a moment and continued.

"It was easier than you think, and it felt good to make her happy. It was what I thought of as a small act of kindness."

Richard thought for a second and asked, "What did you mean?" Steve looked at Richard's puzzled expression.

"About what?" asked Steve.

"You said that you learned a lesson?" Richard inquired.

"I included Abby. It meant so much to her that she went home and told her family about it. She cried."   Steve smiled. "Her mother called the school and told them what I had done. They said they wanted to thank me for my kindness and that Abby was happy."

"A small act of kindness isn't small at all," Steve told Richard.

"I want to make Alexandra happy too, just like Abby!" said Richard.

The next day, Richard invited Alexandra to sit with him during lunch. He asked her about Poland and what games she played there. "I liked to play baseball," Alexandra said. "I was a pitcher," she added.

"You should play with us!" Richard said. He looked around the table.

"She should play with us, we should include her."

At recess, Richard cheered for Alexandra. She was a good pitcher. The other boys cheered too. Alexandra was happy.

When Richard went inside after recess his teacher said, "Richard, I saw what you did for Alexandra today. It was very kind."

"Yes", replied Richard, smiling back at his teacher. "It was a small act of kindness that wasn't small at all."

Printed in the United States
By Bookmasters